NASTY ways to GO

ROAR!

FINISHED BY FOOD

by Charis Mather

BEARPORT PUBLISHING

Minneapolis, Minnesota

Credits
All images are courtesy of Shutterstock.com, unless otherwise specified. With thanks to Getty Images, Thinkstock Photo, and iStockphoto. Background texture throughout – Abstracto. Gravestone throughout – MaryValery. Front Cover – x. 4–5 – Master1305, LightField Studios. 6–7 – Everett Collection. 8–9 – Scott Latham. 10–11 – Pchelintseva Natalya. 12–13 – Anna Krivitskaya, Mehmet Cetin, Jarous, Anydudl. 14–15 – Ysbrand Cosijn. 16–17 – rukxstockphoto, Dann77. 18–19 – PeopleImages.com - Yuri A. 20–21 – gowithstock, Nicole M Iizuka, alexzrv, LightField Studios, robuart. 22–23 – Brent Hofacker, HC FOTOSTUDIO, Look Studio, Kseniya Maruk.

Bearport Publishing Company Product Development Team
President: Jen Jenson; Director of Product Development: Spencer Brinker; Managing Editor: Allison Juda; Associate Editor: Naomi Reich; Senior Designer: Colin O'Dea; Associate Designer: Elena Klinkner; Associate Designer: Kayla Eggert; Product Development Specialist: Anita Stasson

Library of Congress Cataloging-in-Publication Data is available at www.loc.gov or upon request from the publisher.

ISBN: 979-8-88822-006-1 (hardcover)
ISBN: 979-8-88822-191-4 (paperback)
ISBN: 979-8-88822-321-5 (ebook)

For more information, write to Bearport Publishing, 5357 Penn Avenue South, Minneapolis, MN 55419.

CONTENTS

LAST MEALS, STRANGE DEATHS

We eat to stay alive. However, some unlucky people have found themselves finished by food.

Let's find out about some of the people who met their death after a **feast.**

PYTHAGORAS

FINISHED BY: BEANS

Pythagoras was known for his interesting ideas. However, not everyone agreed with him.

One day, Pythagoras was chased by a group of people who were angry about his ideas.

Then, Pythagoras came across a field of beans.

He believed hurting bean plants was wrong. He would not run through the field to get away.

Poor Pythagoras was killed by the angry crowd.

If only they cared about Pythagoras as much as he cared about beans!

MRS. TROFFEA

FINISHED BY: BREAD AND BALLET

Mrs. Troffea had always been normal. Until one day when something very strange happened.

Mrs. Troffea started dancing.

Once she started, she could not stop.

Mrs. Troffea died from **exhaustion** a week later.

And Mrs. Troffea wasn't alone. Her dancing spread to hundreds of people.

Many others died, too.

Some people thought Mrs. Troffea had eaten **poisonous** bread.

Can bread make you dance until you drop?

HENRY PURCELL

FINISHED BY: CHOCOLATE

Henry Purcell was a great **composer**. But his music came to a sweet end.

His death was blamed on chocolate.

During his time, chocolate was **expensive.**

Rich people went to places called cocoa houses to drink hot chocolate.

Henry had plenty of money because of his job.

So, he visited a cocoa house to try hot chocolate.

Shortly after, Henry died. Did he drink a bad cup of cocoa?

Henry should have spent his money on something else!

KING ADOLF FREDERICK

FINISHED BY: A FEAST

King Adolf Frederick of Sweden was going to cut back on some foods during **Lent**.

He wanted to eat many of the foods he liked before it started.

The king ate a huge meal. He had lobster, fish eggs, sour cabbage, fish, and 14 cream-filled buns.

King Adolf ate too much. He died shortly after. At least his last meal was a good one!

NASTY WAYS TO GO

Pythagoras, Mrs. Troffea, Henry, and King Adolf were all finished by food. Who had the most tasteless death?

Pythagoras

Mrs. Troffea

Henry Purcell

King Adolf Frederick

They battled beans, danced to death, drank killer chocolate, and fed to the finish.

Those are some nasty ways to go!

GLOSSARY

composer someone who writes music, especially as their job

exhaustion the state of being very tired and having little or no energy

expensive costing a lot of money

feast a big meal with different dishes

Lent a time of year leading up to the Christian festival of Easter when some people choose not to eat certain foods

poisonous having something that can harm or kill

INDEX